OUR
GRE★T
STATES

WHAT'S GREAT ABOUT
MAINE?

✳ Andrea Wang

LERNER PUBLICATIONS ✳ MINNEAPOLIS

CONTENTS

MAINE
WELCOMES YOU! ✳ 4

ACADIA NATIONAL PARK ✳ 6

MAINE MARITIME MUSEUM ✳ 8

BAXTER STATE PARK ✳ 10

MOOSEHEAD LAKE REGION ✳ 12

MACHIAS WILD BLUEBERRY FESTIVAL ✳ 14

Copyright © 2015
by Lerner Publishing Group, Inc.

Content Consultant: Polly Welts Kaufman,
Associate Professor of History (PT), University
of Southern Maine

Lerner Publications Company
A division of Lerner Publishing Group, Inc.
241 First Avenue North
Minneapolis, MN 55401 USA

For reading levels and more information, look
up this title at www.lernerbooks.com.

Main body text set in ITC Franklin Gothic Std
Book Condensed 12/15.
Typeface provided by Adobe Systems.

Library of Congress Cataloging-in-Publication
Data

Wang, Andrea.
   What's great about Maine? / by Andrea
Wang.
      pages cm. — (Our great states)
   Includes bibliographical references and
index.
   ISBN 978-1-4677-3855-2 (lib. bdg. :
alk. paper) — ISBN 978-1-4677-6079-9
(pbk.) — ISBN 978-1-4677-6257-1 (EB
pdf)
   1. Maine—Description and travel—
Juvenile literature. I. Title.
F19.3.W36 2015
974.1—dc23   2014024053

Manufactured in the United States of America
1 – PC – 12/31/14

SUNDAY RIVER SKI RESORT ✳ 16

COASTAL MAINE
BOTANICAL GARDENS ✳ 18

MONHEGAN ISLAND ✳ 20

PORTLAND ✳ 22

BOOTHBAY HARBOR ✳ 24

MAINE BY MAP ✳ 26
MAINE FACTS ✳ 28
GLOSSARY ✳ 30
FURTHER INFORMATION ✳ 31
INDEX ✳ 32

MAINE Welcomes You!

Maine's beauty attracts visitors from all around the world. People come to experience nature in every season. The snowy winters are perfect for skiers and snowmobilers. Hiking, boating, and camping are popular in the summer. In the fall, people enjoy the amazing colors of the tree leaves. From the rocky Atlantic coast to the Appalachian Mountains, adventure waits around every bend. Read on to discover ten places that make the Pine Tree State great. Then grab your gear and go!

Explore Maine's shores and all the places in between. Just turn the page to find out all about the PINE TREE STATE. >

CANADA

Saint John River

CANADA

Miles
0   20   40
0 20 40 60
Kilometers

N

CANADA

Baxter State Park

Mount Katahdin
(5,267 feet/
1,606 m)

LONGFELLOW MOUNTAINS

Moosehead Lake

Kennebec River

Penobscot River

Saint Croix River

Androscoggin River

Bangor

Schoodic Peninsula

Augusta

Auburn Lewiston

Brunswick

Acadia National Park

Mount Desert Island

NEW HAMPSHIRE

Portland

Biddeford

South Portland

Isle au Haut

Scarborough

Monhegan Island

Sanford

Saco

ATLANTIC OCEAN
(GULF OF MAINE)

Portsmouth

ACADIA NATIONAL PARK

> Explore the many different ecosystems of Acadia National Park. This park lies on the Atlantic Ocean coast. There are shorelines, mountains, and marshes. Waves crash into a small cavern at Thunder Hole. Listen for a noise like a clap of thunder when the waves hit the cave. At low tide, check out the tide pools at the Bar Island sandbar. Crabs, starfish, and sea urchins are often easy to spot. Next, relax on a horse-drawn carriage ride. It will take you on a tour through the park's forests and across stone bridges. You'll get a nice view of the ocean as you ride.

You've heard of a webcam. But have you heard of a scuba cam? Hop on a Dive-In Theater boat cruise. Watch on-screen as a scuba diver collects lobsters and other sea creatures from the ocean floor. Touch the wildlife the diver brings aboard during a fun show-and-tell session.

Cadillac Mountain is another part of the park. Visit between October and March. Climb to the top of the mountain before dawn. You'll be the first person in the country to see the sunrise!

The waves at Thunder Hole can splash as high as 40 feet (12 meters) into the air!

MAINE'S FISHING INDUSTRY

Fishing is a big business in Maine. Approximately twenty-six thousand people work in the fishing industry. Lobsters bring in the most money. Maine harvests more lobsters than any other state. But overfishing is a big concern. This happens when too many fish or lobsters are caught. Maine has put a limit on the number of fish people can catch. There are also laws about which lobsters can be caught. Fishers can only catch lobsters of a certain size. And they cannot catch egg-bearing female lobsters.

MAINE MARITIME MUSEUM

> Visit a historic shipyard at the Maine Maritime Museum in Bath. This shipyard is right next to the Kennebec River. It has been home to shipbuilding for more than two hundred years. One of the world's largest wooden ships, the *Wyoming*, was built here. Walk through a metal sculpture of the *Wyoming*. Six tall masts loom above the ship. Each one is 177 feet (54 m) tall!

Inside the museum, examine the more than twenty thousand artifacts. The museum is home to ship models, tools, and a working steam engine. See strange items. You'll find jewelry made out of human hair and a jar of whale oil.

Dive into the life of a sailor at the museum. Blow the horn and the whistle as you pretend to pilot a river tugboat. Outside, learn how to tie knots on the 50-foot (15 m) pirate play ship. You can watch boats being built in the boat shop. Or even watch a boat launch. The museum also offers boat tours down the river.

View old lobster fishing equipment at the Maine Maritime Museum's lobstering exhibit.

Push the bars of the capstan, a machine that once hoisted sails, inside the Maine Maritime Museum.

BAXTER STATE PARK

> See Maine's tallest point in Baxter State Park. Here, the peak of Mount Katahdin rises 5,267 feet (1,606 m) into the air. Hiking in Baxter State Park is like walking through history. Some of the trails here are more than one hundred years old! As you hike, keep your eyes peeled for wildlife. You can borrow a pack from the park's visitor center. It has binoculars, dip nets, bug boxes, and books inside. Use them to identify the animals and plants you see.

Baxter State Park can't be explored in one day. It has more than 200,000 acres (80,900 hectares) of forest and wilderness! Camp at one of the park's twelve campgrounds. Cool off with a dip in the water at Ledge Falls during your stay. Or rent a canoe and a fishing pole. Can you hook a trout for dinner? In the summer, there are kids' programs each Saturday morning. Learn cool facts about bats, birds, and bugs.

Moose, bears, bobcats, and more live in Baxter State Park.

MOUNT KATAHDIN

Mount Katahdin's name comes from an American Indian word. The Penobscot American Indians named the mountain *Katahdin*, which means "greatest mountain." The Penobscot people are one of five American Indian nations in Maine. You can visit the home of the Penobscot Nation on Indian Island. This island is on the Penobscot River.

MOOSEHEAD LAKE REGION

> There are more than twenty-five hundred lakes and ponds in Maine. Moosehead Lake is the largest. It spreads across 117 square miles (303 square kilometers). Look at a map of the lake. Can you spot the shape of a moose's head?

During the warmer months, go on a moose safari to scout for moose. Breakneck Ridge Farm is also in the region. Tour the farm for a view of the many buffalo living here. A hayride will take you to the farm's sugar house. Taste maple syrup and see how it's made. Next, get wet on a whitewater rafting trip down the Kennebec River. For a more relaxing boat ride, cruise across Moosehead Lake in a steamboat or canoe. On a clear day, you can see Mount Katahdin in the distance.

In winter, try the traditional Maine hobby of ice fishing. Skim across the snow on a dogsled ride. Then head over to Greenville Junction West Cove. Here, watch race cars and trucks speed around an ice track. Or go snowmobiling. It is one of Maine's most popular winter sports.

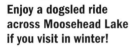

Enjoy a dogsled ride across Moosehead Lake if you visit in winter!

MAINE'S MAJOR RIVERS

Glaciers once covered all of Maine. As the ice melted, many lakes formed. Moosehead Lake is the source of the Kennebec River, one of the major rivers in Maine. The five major rivers of Maine are the Saint John, Saint Croix, Penobscot, Kennebec, and Androscoggin Rivers. These rivers are important to Maine's economy. In the past, they provided transportation for the logging industry, powered mills, and helped the shipbuilding industry. The rivers generate hydroelectric power and attract visitors to the state.

MACHIAS WILD BLUEBERRY FESTIVAL

> The town of Machias is known for its blueberries. The town has even earned the nickname Blueberry Capital of the World! Celebrate this delicious fruit at the Machias Wild Blueberry Festival in August. Show off a blue costume in the children's parade. Switch to racing sneakers for the Blueberry Fun Run. Do you like to cook? Enter your best blueberry dessert in the cooking contest. Then stuff your face in the blueberry pie-eating contest! Are you thirsty? Wash down all of that pie with a refreshing blueberry soda.

The festival's Kid Zone has lots of activities. Have your face painted, see a puppet show, or build a birdhouse. Go on a blueberry farm tour at Welch Farm. Find out how blueberries are grown and harvested. Buy fresh-picked blueberries at the farm, or pick your own!

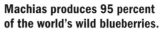
Machias produces 95 percent of the world's wild blueberries.

WILD BLUEBERRY LAND

WILD BLUEBERRY LAND

GIFTS

BLUEBERRY

Famous Ice Cream

Enter the blueberry pie-eating contest at the Machias Wild Blueberry Festival.

SUNDAY RIVER SKI RESORT

> Do you love to play in the snow? Then the Sunday River ski resort in Newry is the place to go. The resort receives an average of 167 inches (424 centimeters) of snow each year. There are 135 trails to explore. Never skied before? A ski school program can teach you. Other winter activities include snow tubing, ice-skating, snowshoeing, and cross-country skiing. In the evening, attend a show. Magicians, jugglers, and fire dancers perform. On most winter weekends, enjoy the display of fireworks above South Ridge lodge.

Sunday River is also full of fun summer activities. Hike the mountain trails, play regular or disc golf, or ride a mountain bike through the woods. For more thrills, bounce 20 feet (6 m) in the air on the bungee trampoline. Or soar through the trees on a zip-line tour. Return to the ground and relax in one of the resort's heated swimming pools.

Sunday River skiing lessons will prepare you for the beginner trails.

MAINE'S MOUNTAINS

Maine has three major land regions: the Atlantic Ocean coastal lowlands, the central uplands, and the Longfellow Mountains. The Longfellow Mountains are an extension of the White Mountains in New Hampshire. Both the Longfellow Mountains and the White Mountains belong to the Appalachian Mountain system. The Appalachian Mountain system runs from Newfoundland in Canada all the way down to Alabama in the United States!

COASTAL MAINE BOTANICAL GARDENS

> If you love exploring nature, don't miss the Coastal Maine Botanical Gardens in Boothbay. There's almost always something in bloom. Follow the trails past waterfalls, along rock ledges, and through the woods. Look for the sculptures scattered throughout the gardens. Can you find the giant pinecone?

The Fairy House Village is a magical spot in the gardens. Dozens of tiny houses are nestled among the trees. With a handful of twigs, bark, and moss, you can build your very own fairy house. Stop by the Children's Garden for more fairy fun. Slip into some wings and dance your way through the garden maze. Listen to stories and watch a puppet show in the Story Barn. You can also climb into a tree house, cross a rope bridge, and pet the stone dragons.

Coneflowers are just one kind of flower you'll find at the Coastal Maine Botanical Gardens.

Wind through paths to see flowers and houses in the Coastal Maine Botanical Gardens Children's Garden.

MONHEGAN ISLAND

> There are no cars or paved roads on the tiny island of Monhegan. You can only get to this rocky island by boat. Hike along some of the tallest ocean cliffs off the coast of Maine. Don't forget your binoculars! Monhegan is a haven for birds and birdwatchers. Spot harbor seals sunning on the rocks. The rusty remains of an old shipwreck lie on the rocks at Lobster Cove. The tugboat ran ashore in 1948. You can climb down to the wreck and get a close-up look.

The rugged beauty of Monhegan has attracted artists since the late 1800s. Visit artists' studios or the Monhegan museum to see artwork and historical items. The museum is located in the old Monhegan Light Station. There, you can admire the 47-foot-tall (14 m) lighthouse. Or stop in at the one-room schoolhouse. It's still a working school!

EXPLORER JOHN SMITH

In 1614, English explorer Captain John Smith landed on Monhegan Island. Monhegan Island was Smith's headquarters while he explored the coast of Maine. He made accurate maps of the coastline from Massachusetts to Penobscot Bay in Maine. During this voyage, he named the area New England.

View the peregrine falcons and other birds that stop on Monhegan Island.

PORTLAND

> Portland is Maine's largest city. Visit the Portland Observatory. It is the last working maritime signal station in the United States. Climb the 103 steps to the lantern deck of the lighthouse. From here, you can see Portland Head Light, a large white lighthouse. It sits on the coast of Casco Bay in the Gulf of Maine.

Spend a day exploring the Children's Museum & Theatre of Maine in Portland. Play at the Have a Ball! exhibit. Build your own ramps. Then roll balls down them to explore the science of motion. Next, run the town at the Our Town exhibit. Pretend to fix a car, deliver mail, or cook food in Coco's diner.

Don't forget to put on an act at the Dress-Up Theatre! Watch other children put on a play. Or create your own! Costumes for dressing up and props for acting are available. If you'd rather have a part behind the curtain, head for the sound and light booth. Choose sounds for your play. Light up the stage with different colors!

Pretend to do your own grocery shopping at the Children's Museum & Theatre of Maine in Portland.

BOOTHBAY HARBOR

> Boothbay Harbor is both a town and a body of water. On a whale-watching cruise, you might see six types of whales that migrate to this area. If you're lucky, you might spot a whale jumping out of the water.

A different cruise takes you to a colony of Atlantic puffins on Eastern Egg Rock. Puffins may look a bit like penguins. But unlike penguins, puffins can fly. Watch them fly. Or see them dive underwater as they hunt for fish. On both the whale and puffin tours, catch sight of many other marine animals along the way. Seals and dolphins often like to swim with the whales. Come in June to join in Windjammer Days. Watch as sailing ships cruise into Boothbay Harbor.

On land, visit the Maine State Aquarium. Do you dare to touch the sharks? How about sea urchins, horseshoe crabs, or sand dollars? All of these sea creatures and more can be examined in the touch tanks. The aquarium is also home to many unusual lobsters. Lola the lobster has six claws. All lobsters are red, right? No way! See blue and white lobsters. Other colorful sea creatures also live here. Look for red sea anemones and purple sun stars.

See blue lobsters at the
Maine State Aquarium.

YOUR TOP TEN

Now that you've read about
ten awesome things to
see and do in Maine, think
about what your Maine top
ten list would include. What
would you be most excited
for if you were planning a
Maine vacation? Make your
top ten list on a separate
sheet of paper. If you would
like, you can even turn your
list into a book. Illustrate
it with drawings. Or add
pictures from the Internet
or magazines.

MAINE BY MAP

> MAP KEY

⬟ Capital city

◯ City

◯ Point of interest

▲ Highest elevation

–··– International border

–·– State border

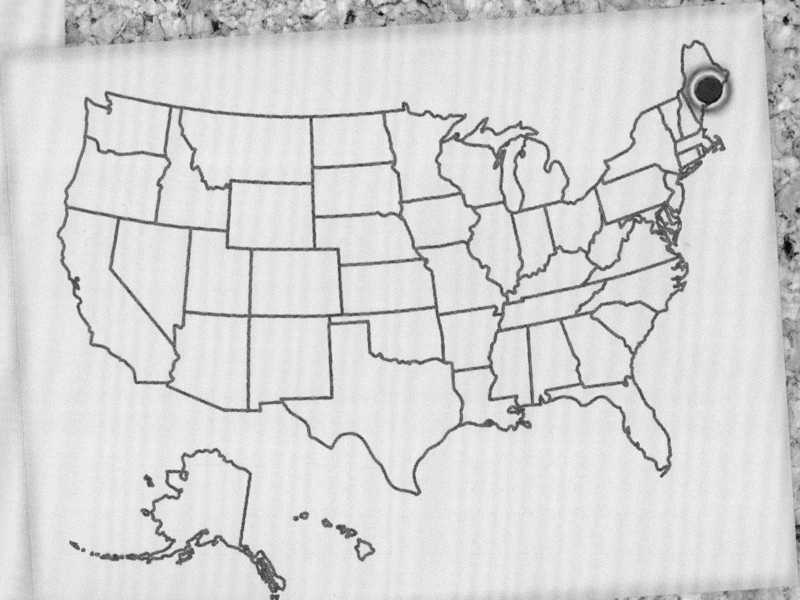

Visit www.lerneresource.com to learn
more about the state flag of Maine.

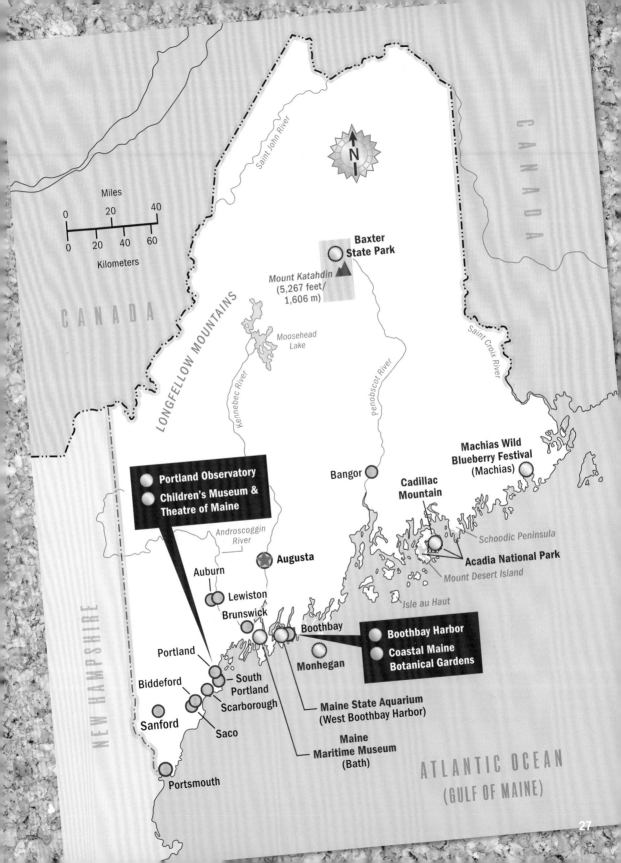

Miles
0   20   40

0   20   40   60
Kilometers

CANADA

CANADA

Saint John River

N

Baxter
State Park

Mount Katahdin
(5,267 feet/
1,606 m)

Moosehead
Lake

LONGFELLOW MOUNTAINS

Kennebec River

Penobscot River

Saint Croix River

Machias Wild
Blueberry Festival
(Machias)

Bangor

Cadillac
Mountain

Schoodic Peninsula

Acadia National Park

Mount Desert Island

Portland Observatory

Children's Museum &
Theatre of Maine

Androscoggin
River

Augusta

Auburn

Lewiston

Brunswick

Boothbay

Boothbay Harbor

Coastal Maine
Botanical Gardens

Isle au Haut

Monhegan

NEW HAMPSHIRE

Portland

Biddeford

South
Portland

Scarborough

Maine State Aquarium
(West Boothbay Harbor)

Sanford

Saco

Maine
Maritime Museum
(Bath)

ATLANTIC OCEAN
(GULF OF MAINE)

Portsmouth

MAINE FACTS

NICKNAME: Pine Tree State

SONG: "State of Maine Song" by Roger Vinton Snow

MOTTO: *Dirigo* (Latin for "I Lead")

FLOWER: eastern white pine cone and tassel

TREE: eastern white pine

BIRD: black-capped chickadee

ANIMAL: moose

FOOD: blueberry pie

DATE AND RANK OF STATEHOOD: March 15, 1820; the 23rd State

CAPITAL: Augusta

AREA: 33,123 square miles (85,788 sq. km)

AVERAGE JANUARY TEMPERATURE: 15°F (–9°C)

AVERAGE JULY TEMPERATURE: 67°F (19°C)

POPULATION AND RANK: 1,328,302; 41st (2013)

MAJOR CITIES AND POPULATIONS: Portland (66,214), Lewiston (36,460), Bangor (32,817), South Portland (25,088), Auburn (22,972)

NUMBER OF US CONGRESS MEMBERS: 2 representatives; 2 senators

NUMBER OF ELECTORAL VOTES: 4

NATURAL RESOURCES: granite, timber, fish, shellfish, tourmaline

AGRICULTURAL PRODUCTS: potatoes, blueberries, eggs, milk

MANUFACTURED GOODS: ships, paper, wood products, maple syrup, shoes

STATE HOLIDAYS AND CELEBRATIONS: Machias Wild Blueberry Festival, Statehood Day, Acadian Festival (Madawaska)

GLOSSARY

ecosystem: all the living things in a place and their relationship to their environment

exhibit: a display of things for people to look at

glacier: a large, slow-moving piece of ice

hydroelectric: using waterpower to produce electricity

industry: the businesses that provide a particular product or service

maritime: relating to the sea, ships, or navigation

mast: a tall pole on a ship that holds up the sails

migrate: to move from one area to another at a certain time of year

motion: the way something moves

FURTHER INFORMATION

Heinrichs, Ann. *Maine*. New York: Children's Press, 2014. This book is full of facts, photos, and lists about the Pine Tree State.

Maine Fast Facts and Trivia
http://www.50states.com/facts/maine.htm#.U3tiDihy-5Q
Learn fifty fun facts about Maine!

Maine Foliage Kids' Page
http://www.maine.gov/dacf/mfs/projects/fall_foliage/kids/movie.html
Check out this site for forest facts, a tree guide, and a video that explains the science behind Maine's beautiful fall leaves.

Maine Kids
http://www.maine.gov/sos/kids
Visit this site from Maine's secretary of state for facts, online games, and maps of Maine.

Perish, Patrick. *Maine: The Pine Tree State*. Minneapolis: Bellwether Media, 2014. Read more about Maine's history, land, wildlife, and landmarks.

Roop, Connie, and Peter Roop. *The Stormy Adventure of Abbie Burgess, Lighthouse Keeper*. Minneapolis: Graphic Universe, 2011. This exciting graphic novel transports you to a lighthouse on Matinicus Rock, Maine, in 1856.

INDEX

Acadia National Park, 6
Appalachian Mountains, 4, 17
Atlantic Ocean, 6, 17

Baxter State Park, 10
Boothbay Harbor, 24
Breakneck Ridge Farm, 12

Cadillac Mountain, 6
Children's Museum & Theatre of Maine, 22
Coastal Maine Botanical Gardens, 18

Eastern Egg Rock, 24

Indian Island, 11

Kennebec River, 8, 12, 13

Ledge Falls, 10
Longfellow Mountains, 17

Machias Wild Blueberry Festival, 14
Maine Maritime Museum, 8
Maine State Aquarium, 24
maps, 5, 27
Monhegan Island, 20
Moosehead Lake, 12, 13
Mount Katahdin, 10, 11, 12

Penobscot River, 11, 13
Portland, 22
Portland Observatory, 22

Smith, John, 20
Sunday River Ski Resort, 16

Thunder Hole, 6

Welch Farm, 14
Wyoming, 8

PHOTO ACKNOWLEDGMENTS

The images in this book are used with the permission of: © Richard Semik/Shutterstock Images, p. 1; NASA, pp. 2–3; © Shutterstock Images, pp. 4, 11 (bottom), 25; © kurdistan/Shutterstock Images, pp. 4–5; © Laura Westlund/Independent Picture Service, pp. 5 (top), 27; © lightphoto/Shutterstock Images, pp. 6–7; © Zack Frank/Shutterstock Images, p. 7 (left); © Andrey Starostin/Shutterstock Images, p. 7 (right); © Leena Robinson/Shutterstock Images, pp. 8–9; © John Elk III/Alamy, p. 9 (top); © Jeff Greenberg/Alamy, p. 9 (bottom); © Andrea Pelletier/Thinkstock, pp. 10–11, 11 (top); © Jeff Schultes/Shutterstock Images, pp. 12–13, 24–25; © Sergey Krasnoshchokov/Shutterstock Images, p. 13 (top); Public Domain, p. 13 (bottom); © Andre Jenny Stock Connection Worldwide/Newscom, pp. 14–15; © Maxpro/Shutterstock Images, p. 15 (top); © Spirit of America/Shutterstock Images, p. 15 (bottom); © Zdenek Krchak/Shutterstock Images, pp. 16–17; © Alaska Stock/Design Pics/SuperStock, p. 17 (left); © Dave Allen Photography/Shutterstock Images, p. 17 (right); © Pat & Chuck Blackley/Alamy, pp. 18–19, 19 (left); © Candia Baxter/Shutterstock Images, p. 19 (right); © Geri Lynn Smith/Shutterstock Images, pp. 20–21; © Tony Baggett/Thinkstock, p. 20; © Chris Hill/Shutterstock Images, p. 21; © Gary Yim/Shutterstock Images, p. 22; © Christine B Miller/Shutterstock Images, pp. 22–23; © Joel Page/AP Images, p. 23; © Francesco de Marco/Shutterstock Images, p. 24; © nicoolay/iStockphoto, p. 26; © Marie C Fields/Shutterstock Images, p. 29 (top right); © Al Mueller/Shutterstock Images, p. 29 (top left); © Phil Reid/Shutterstock Images, p. 29 (bottom right); © KWJ Photo Art/Shutterstock Images, p. 29 (bottom left).

Cover: © Daniel J. Grenier/Moment/Getty Images (snowshoes); © iStockphoto.com/TVAllen_CDI (blueberries); © Baumsaway/istock/Thinkstock (lighthouse); © Laura Westlund/Independent Picture Service (map); © iStockphoto.com/fpm (seal); © iStockphoto.com/vicm (pushpins); © iStockphoto.com/benz190 (corkboard).